I Never
Say
I'm Thankful,
But I Am

by Jane Belk Moncure
illustrated by Frances Hook

THE CHILD'S WORLD

ELGIN, ILLINOIS 60120

Distributed by Childrens Press, 1224 West Van Buren Street, Chicago, Illinois 60607.

Library of Congress Cataloging in Publication Data

Moncure, Jane Belk.
  I never say I'm thankful, but I am.

  SUMMARY: A child thinks about all the things for which he is grateful.
  [1. Gratitude—Fiction] I. Hook, Frances. II. Title.
PZ7.M739Iad   [E]   78-21577
ISBN 0-89565-023-1

I Never
Say
I'm Thankful,
But I Am

by Jane Belk Moncure
illustrated by Frances Hook

I am thankful for my family
at Thanksgiving time
and other holiday times.
But, most of the time, no one talks about it.
Even though I feel thankful,
I hardly ever say it out loud.

I feel it when Mom helps me.
Maybe she feels it when I help her.

I feel it when Dad fixes my bike.
Maybe he feels it when I help him
paint the fence.

My Granddad helps me make things.
I think he knows how thankful I feel.

My Grandma listens when I'm full of things
to tell her.
When I'm sad, she understands.

I never say I'm thankful for my brother,
but I am.
Of course I'm not thankful
when we fight
or when he teases me
and calls me names.
But once he fixed my wagon.
He even helped me paint it.

I never say I'm thankful for my friends,
but I am.
I am lonely when a friend moves away.

I never say I'm thankful for my dog,
even though he's my best pal.

I never say I'm thankful
for crickets and frogs.
But I let them go
so they can find their way home.

I never say I'm thankful for the beach,
or the waves,

or the mountains of sand,
or the sea gulls racing the wind,

or a pinchy crab hiding under a shell.

No, I hardly ever say I'm thankful,
but I am.

About the Artist

Frances Hook was educated at the Pennsylvania Museum School of Art in Philadelphia, Pennsylvania. She and her husband, Richard Hook, worked together as a free-lance art team for many years, until his death. Within the past 15 years, Mrs. Hook has moved more and more into the field of book illustrating.

Mrs. Hook has a unique ability for capturing the moods and emotions of children. She has this to say about her work. "Over the years, I have centered my attention on children. I've done many portraits of children. I use children in the neighborhood for my models. I never use professional models."

A great admirer of Mary Cassatt, an American Impressionist, Mrs. Hook enjoys doing fine art as well as commercial work.

About the Author

Jane Belk Moncure, author of many books and stories for young children, is a graduate of Virginia Commonwealth University and Columbia University. She has taught nursery, kindergarten and primary children in Europe and America.

Mrs. Moncure has taught early childhood education while serving on the faculties of Virginia Commonwealth University and the University of Richmond. She was the first president of the Virginia Association for Early Childhood Education and has been recognized widely for her services to young children.

She is married to Dr. James A. Moncure, Vice President of Elon College, and lives in Burlington, North Carolina.